HEINEMANN MATHEMATICS P7

Reinforcement Sheets

Heinemann Mathematics P7 is intended for use with children
- working in Key Stage 2 or Key Stage 3, mainly at Levels 4 and 5, of the National Curriculum (England and Wales)
- working in Key Stage 2, mainly at Levels 4 and 5, of the Common Curriculum (Northern Ireland) and
- completing Level D and moving into Level E of Mathematics 5–14 (Scotland).

Heinemann Educational Publishers
Halley Court, Jordan Hill, Oxford OX2 8EJ
a division of Reed Educational & Professional Publishing Ltd

OXFORD MELBOURNE AUCKLAND
JOHANNESBURG BLANTYRE GABORONE
IBADAN PORTSMOUTH (NH) USA CHICAGO

ISBN 0 435 02250 4

© Scottish Primary Mathematics Group 1996
First published 1996
05 04 03 02
10 9 8 7

Writing Team
John T Blair
Ian K Clark
Aileen P Duncan
Percy W Farren
Archie MacCallum
Myra A Pearson
Dorothy S Simpson
John W Thayers
David K Thomson

Designed and produced by Oxprint
Printed in the UK by Athenæum Press Ltd, Gateshead, Tyne & Wear

Introduction

- This booklet contains 32 photocopiable reinforcement sheets designed to provide further practice in selected topics for children using Heinemann Mathematics P7.

- Each sheet is referenced from a specific page of Heinemann Mathematics P7 Textbook or Workbook and is designed to supplement the mathematics of the section from which it is referenced. For example, page 10 of the Textbook carries the symbol **R4**

    to indicate that reinforcement sheet 4 is available to provide further practice in the aspect dealt with in that section, ie division by 10, 100, 1000 and multiples of 10 by 2 to 10.

- The top right-hand corner of each reinforcement sheet states the mathematical topic and the associated Textbook and Workbook pages. The reference appears on the last page only — in the example shown here, Textbook page 10.

    For example,

Division: by 10, 100, 1000 and multiples of 10 by 2 to 10
Heinemann Mathematics P7 Textbook, pages 9 and 10

- A list of the sheets, with the mathematical topics they cover and references to Textbook and Workbook pages, is given on the next page.

- The *Teacher's Notes* list reinforcement sheets in the Overview section for each mathematical topic. The 'R' symbol described above also appears beside the notes for a core page (or the final core page in a sequence of pages), which has an associated reinforcement sheet. Curriculum references and teaching notes are the same as for the core pages, and can be found in the *Teacher's Notes*.

- Each sheet is intended to be used *selectively* with those children who show a need for some extra practice over and above that provided in the core materials.

    There is no advantage in using the sheets routinely with children who have already mastered the work. They would be better engaged in using the Extension Textbook, the Problem Solving Activities in the Assessment and Resources Pack, or in tackling a new topic.

    The sheets are not designed to assist those pupils whose understanding of the topic is so poor that they really require further teaching before engaging in more practice.

- In most cases the reinforcement sheets continue the *context* of the core section to which they relate. This is intended to make it easier to integrate them with on-going work when supplementary examples are required for some children.

- Some of the sheets have a fill-in format. A 'pencil' symbol appears beside the number of the sheet in these cases. **6**✏

- The only materials required are calculators, protractors, coloured pencils, scissors and glue.

- Answers are provided at the end of this booklet.

Mathematical content

Reinforcement sheet	Topic	Referenced from
1 Droids at work	Mental addition and subtraction	Workbook page 1
2 *Zarco*'s command centre	Rounding to the nearest 1000, 100	Textbook page 5
3 Work camps	Multiplication: by 10, 100, 1000 and by multiples of 10, 100	Textbook page 8
4 Lineum crystals	Division: by 10, 100, 1000 and multiples of 10 by 2 to 10	Textbook page 10
5 Transporters	Place value: hundreds of millions	Textbook page 14
6 Fruit and veg	Division: calculator, exact remainders	Textbook page 16
7 Droids on Planet Ag	Calculator, checking answers	Textbook page 18
8 Mosaics	Fractions: equivalence, simplification	Textbook page 21
9 Kitbits Shapes packs	Fractions: of a set, mixed, improper	Textbook page 22
10 Kitbits colourama	Fractions: addition and subtraction	Textbook page 25
11 *Orlando*	Decimals: notation and place value	Textbook page 30
12 All at sea	Decimals: first and second places, addition and subtraction	Textbook page 32
13 Team games	Decimals: multiplication	Textbook page 35
14 Children's club	Decimals: division	Textbook page 39
15 Souvenirs	Decimals: approximation and estimation	Textbook page 41
16 Gifts	Decimals: approximation and estimation	Workbook page 8
17 Theatre outing	Decimals: calculator	Textbook page 43
18 Farm kits	Percentages: link with fractions, calculations based on 10%	Textbook page 47
19 Taking orders	Percentages: fractions as percentages	Textbook page 49
20 Another code competition	Percentages: fractions, decimals	Textbook page 50
21 Plant experiments	Pattern: formulae using symbols	Textbook page 55
22 Small creatures	Length: millimetres	Textbook page 68
23 Walled garden	Length: drawing to scale	Workbook page 15
24 Label designs	Area: composite shapes	Textbook page 76
25 Lick 'n' stickers	Area: right-angled triangles	Textbook page 77
26 Doodles	Area: composite shapes	Workbook page 26
27 Running speeds	Speed: metres per second, kilometres per hour	Textbook page 86
28 Hotel Sublimo	Time: 24-hour clock, durations	Textbook page 89
29 Weekend in London	Time: 24-hour clock, counting on and counting back	Textbook page 91
30 Angles	Angles: measuring	Textbook page 92
31 Shape talk	2D Shape: sides, angles	Textbook page 102
32 Sponsors for cycle-cross	Handling data: class intervals	Textbook page 114

Droids at work

Mental addition and subtraction
Heinemann Mathematics P7
Textbook pages 1 and 2, Workbook page 1

1

1 Find **mentally**:
  (a) The total number of rods in • container A • container B.
  (b) The difference between the total number of rods in container A and in container B.

2 Add or subtract mentally.
  (a) 23 + 18   (b) 57 − 34   (c) 90 − 28   (d) 54 − 37   (e) 55 + 17
  (f) 22 + 48   (g) 36 − 19   (h) 13 + 48   (i) 45 − 16   (j) 78 + 19
  (k) 41 − 14   (l) 92 − 23   (m) 26 + 65   (n) 54 − 17   (o) 43 + 37

3 Add mentally to find the total number of each type of item.

Item	gloves	helmets	lasers	drills	boots	visors
Green store	40	70	150	160	45	120
Blue store	80	120	60	38	190	98

4

Which droid numbers have a difference of   (a) 30   (b) 100   (c) 150?

5 Add or subtract mentally.
  (a) 64 + 70   (b) 53 + 80   (c) 130 + 69   (d) 60 + 155   (e) 190 + 68
  (f) 130 − 18   (g) 160 − 53   (h) 290 − 52   (i) 200 − 81   (j) 430 − 17
  (k) 86 + 130   (l) 96 + 180   (m) 370 − 53   (n) 140 + 71   (o) 500 − 65

6 Add mentally in the easiest order. Write your order.
  (a) 6 + 18 + 4   (b) 3 + 29 + 7   (c) 18 + 21 + 9   (d) 13 + 7 + 18
  (e) 25 + 30 + 15   (f) 19 + 31 + 16   (g) 26 + 16 + 14   (h) 10 + 19 + 31

Zarco's command centre

Rounding to the nearest 1000, 100
Heinemann Mathematics P7
Textbook page 5

2

1 These gauges are in *Zarco's* command centre.
Write the number on each gauge **to the nearest thousand**.

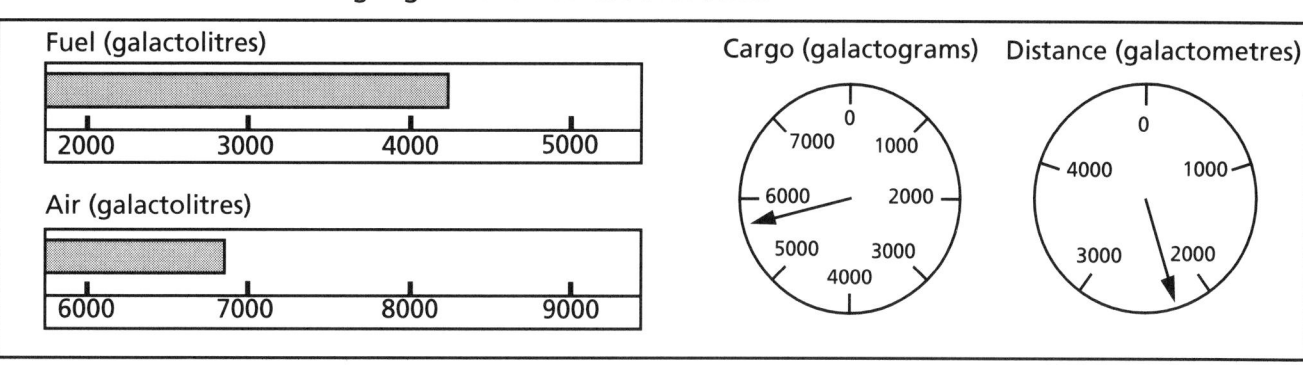

2 Round **to the nearest thousand**.
   (a) 4300   (b) 7900   (c) 2628   (d) 9360   (e) 7555   (f) 12 855
   (g) 21 498   (h) 17 506   (i) 34 455   (j) 61 755   (k) 27 556   (l) 43 192

3 **To the nearest hundred galactolitres**, write the volume of   (a) fuel   (b) air.

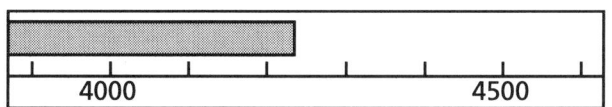 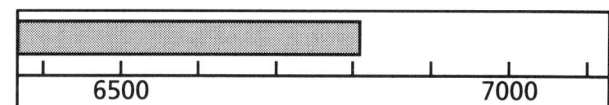

4 Round **to the nearest hundred**.
   (a) 2409   (b) 8355   (c) 2761   (d) 7091   (e) 15 308
   (f) 32 345   (g) 19 649   (h) 66 666   (i) 41 450   (j) 70 025

| Varum | Ambal | Rodon | Varum |
| 1832 rods | 3109 rods | 1937 rods | 4215 rods |

| Ambal | Rodon |
| 5716 rods | 3809 rods |

5 By rounding **to the nearest thousand**,
estimate the total number of
   (a) Varum rods   (b) Ambal rods   (c) Rodon rods.

6 Round **to the nearest thousand** to estimate:
   (a) 2194 + 3872   (b) 5843 + 2075   (c) 6984 − 2125
   (d) 12 731 − 5608   (e) 3127 + 28 099   (f) 2155 + 14 762
   (g) 19 288 − 7905   (h) 27 214 − 7050   (i) 38 550 − 6645

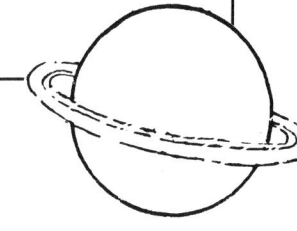

Work camps

Multiplication by 10, 100, 1000 and by multiples of 10, 100
Heinemann Mathematics P7
Textbook pages 7 and 8

3

1. At the workcamps on Stobal, 10 workers live in each cabin. How many workers live in
   (a) 25 cabins (b) 149 cabins (c) 260 cabins?

2. Multiply each number by 10.
   (a) 43 (b) 95 (c) 138 (d) 104 (e) 600

3. Each worker pays 100 credits to live in a cabin. How many credits altogether would be paid by
   (a) 36 workers (b) 127 workers (c) 340 workers?

4. Multiply each number by 100.
   (a) 65 (b) 20 (c) 407 (d) 820 (e) 243 (f) 700

5. Workers use phone cards to phone home to Earth. They pay 1 credit for every 1000 phone units. How many phone units can they buy for
   (a) 58 credits (b) 102 credits (c) 480 credits?

6. Multiply each number by 1000.
   (a) 72 (b) 89 (c) 205 (d) 362 (e) 490 (f) 273

   > 3 times 18 energy packs
   > 3 tens + 3 eights
   > = 30 + 24
   > = 54 energy packs

7. Each worker is given 18 energy packs. How many packs are given to
   (a) 6 workers (b) 8 workers?

8. Find mentally.
   (a) 4 × 17 (b) 15 × 5 (c) 6 × 13
   (d) 19 × 2 (e) 9 × 12 (f) 17 × 7

9. There are 40 food packs in each cabin. How many food packs are in
   (a) 3 cabins (b) 5 cabins
   (c) 8 cabins (d) 9 cabins?

10. Find mentally.
    (a) 4 × 30 (b) 7 × 60 (c) 80 × 9 (d) 6 × 40 (e) 8 × 70
    (f) 4 × 300 (g) 5 × 700 (h) 400 × 4 (i) 600 × 6 (j) 500 × 8

11. Find mentally.
    (a) 20 × 40 (b) 60 × 30 (c) 70 × 70 (d) 50 × 80 (e) 90 × 60

12. Estimate.
    (a) 43 × 19 (b) 13 × 29 (c) 26 × 18 (d) 38 × 21 (e) 17 × 45